CONNECTICUT

in words and pictures

BY DENNIS B. FRADIN

ILLUSTRATIONS BY RICHARD WAHL

MAPS BY LEN W. MEENTS

Consultant:
    Arthur E. Soderlind
    Consultant
    Social Studies/Independent Schools
    Connecticut State Department of Education

CHILDRENS PRESS ™

CHICAGO

Kent Falls

Library of Congress Cataloging in Publication Data

Fradin, Dennis B.
  Connecticut in words and pictures.

  SUMMARY: A brief introduction to the history,
geography, cities, industries, places of interest,
and famous citizens of the Constitution State.
  1. Connecticut—Juvenile literature. [1. Connecti-
cut] I. Wahl, Richard, 1939- II. Meents, Len W.
III. Title.
F94.3.F7   974.6   79-23292
ISBN 0-516-03907-5

PICTURE ACKNOWLEDGMENTS:
CONNECTICUT DEPARTMENT OF ECONOMIC DEVELOPMENT—cover,
pages 2, 4, 5, 8, 17, 19, 20, 21, 22(bottom right), 26, 29, 31, 33, 34, 37,
38, 39, 40, 42
MUSEUM OF CONNECTICUT HISTORY, CONNECTICUT STATE
LIBRARY, HARTFORD—pages 15, 22(left), 24
COVER—Horse-drawn sleigh in winter

Connecticut

Connecticut (kuh • NET • ih • cut) comes from an Algonkian (al • GAHN • kee • an) Indian phrase. It means *upon the long river* or *on the long tidal river*. The river they meant was the Connecticut River. It divides the state nearly in half. Connecticut is in the northeastern United States, in the area known as *New England.* It is the third smallest state. But it is a beautiful one. It has a rocky seashore. It has hills, lakes, and forests. It has lovely towns. Some are more than 300 years old. Connecticut is also a modern manufacturing state. Many products from silverware to helicopters are made there. And it has much more.

Do you know where the words of the song "Yankee Doodle" were written? Do you know where Revolutionary War hero Nathan Hale was born? Do you know where the first modern sewing machines and clocks were invented? Do you know where the first nuclear-powered submarine was built?

As you will learn, the answer to these questions is Connecticut.

Long before there were people in Connecticut, there were dinosaurs. Their footprints and bones have been found. Near Hartford and Middletown are dinosaur tracks. They were made 200 million years ago.

Dinosaur footprints in Dinosaur State Park

Many Connecticut lakes were formed by glaciers

About one million years ago the Ice Age began. Huge mountains of ice, called *glaciers* (GLAY • shurz), covered Connecticut. The glaciers scooped out large holes from the earth. When the Ice Age ended, the holes filled with water. Many lovely lakes in Connecticut were formed this way.

Long before other people came to Connecticut, Indians lived there. They belonged to the Algonkian family of tribes. The Pequot (PEE • kwat), Niantic (nye • AN • tick), Mohegan (mo • HEE • gan), Saukiog (SAW • kee • og), and Siwanog (SEE • wah • nog) were some of the tribes. As many as 12,000 Indians may have lived in Connecticut.

The Indians of Connecticut lived mainly by hunting and fishing. They made bows and arrows for hunting. They built canoes for fishing. They also grew corn, beans, and tobacco. Their clothing was made of deerskin and beaver furs. Connecticut Indians lived in *wigwams*. These were dome-shaped houses made of poles, tree bark, and grass.

It is thought that Adriaen (AID • ree • an) Block was the first white explorer in Connecticut. Block was a Dutchman. He was from the Netherlands (NEH • ther • landz). In 1614, Block sailed up the Connecticut River. His small boat was called the *Onrust* (meaning "Restless"). Block claimed the land for the Dutch. But the Dutch did not want to settle in Connecticut. They wanted to trade with the Indians for furs. They gave knives, pots, pans, and other items to the Indians. In return the Indians gave them valuable furs. In 1633 the Dutch built a trading post at what is now Hartford.

Adriaen Block's boat, the *Onrust*

Some early Connecticut settlers built homes and other buildings that are still standing today. The Webb House in Wethersfield (top left) was built in 1752. The Old Town Mill in New London was built in 1650. The Buttolph-Williams House in Wethersfield (bottom pictures) was built in 1693.

The English wanted to settle in Connecticut. By the 1630s, English people lived in Massachusetts (mass • ah • CHOO • sets). They had gone to Massachusetts from England. They wanted freedom. Some felt that the Massachusetts government was too strict. They wanted to make a new colony.

In 1632 Englishman Edward Winslow explored the Connecticut Valley. In the 1630s hundreds of English settlers moved from Massachusetts to Connecticut. They built towns in Hartford, Wethersfield, and Windsor. These were called the "Three River Towns" because they were built along the Connecticut River.

The Connecticut settlers cut down trees. They built wooden houses. They shot deer and bears for meat. They used the skins for clothes and blankets. The Indians taught them how to grow corn. These early settlers had a hard life.

In 1636 the Three River Towns joined to form the Connecticut Colony. Citizens held meetings to plan their futures. The Reverend Thomas Hooker was a founder of Hartford. In 1638 he preached a famous sermon. He said that people had to the right to vote for their lawmakers. This sermon was the basis for the *Fundamental Orders*. These laws gave voters the right to elect their officials. Connecticut's Fundamental Orders are often called the "first written constitution."

Other towns—including New London, Saybrook, Farmington, and Fairfield—joined the growing Connecticut Colony.

People in the Connecticut area were called *Yankees*. Some think it was the Dutch who gave them this name.

The Dutch called English settlers "Johnnies." But when
they said "Johnny," it sounded more like *Yankee*.

The Dutch were driven out by the English without
much bloodshed. But the English and the Indians had
brutal battles. The Indians were tricked into selling some
lands. The English just took other lands. The Indians
watched their hunting grounds disappear. Their blood
boiled.

There were small fights between the English and the Indians. In 1636 Indians killed John Oldham, who had founded Wethersfield. A year later, Captain John Mason led an army against the Indians.

On a bright moonlit night the army came to a Pequot Indian village on the Mystic River. Mason and his men crept into the village. A dog barked. An Indian watchman called *"Owanux!"* (oh • WAHN • ux), meaning "Englishmen!" Mason grabbed a torch. He threw it on the roof of a wigwam. The Indian village was soon on fire. Those Indians who tried to escape were shot. As many as 700 Indians may have been murdered by Mason and his men. The rest of the Pequots hid in a swamp. The English tracked them down and killed even more Indians. The English had won what came to be called "The Pequot War."

Years later, the Wampanoag (wahm • pa • NO • ag) chief Metacomet (met • ah • COE • met), known as King Philip, fought for Indian lands. He united Indians from many tribes. The Indians won some battles. Finally, Indians and soldiers met in the Great Swamp Fight near South Kingston, Rhode Island. The Indians were beaten. This was the end of Indian Wars in the Connecticut area.

Today, about 4,000 Indians live in the state.

More settlers came to Connecticut. More towns joined the Connecticut Colony. In 1662 Connecticut officially became an English colony. The king of England gave the Connecticut Colony a charter. Connecticut was one of the thirteen original English colonies. In 1665 New Haven joined the Connecticut Colony.

Their charter gave the people of Connecticut more freedom than people in other colonies. They had more freedom to govern themselves. In 1687 Sir Edmund Andros was made governor of all New England. He planned to limit the people's freedom. Andros came to Hartford. He said that Connecticut must turn over its charter.

Painting of the Charter Oak Tree by C.D.W. Brownell

The charter papers were brought out. Connecticut people were angry. They watched Andros prepare to take over the government. Suddenly someone blew out the candles. The meetinghouse was pitch-black. The charter disappeared. It was said that the papers were hidden in a large tree. This came to be known as the Charter Oak.

Andros did rule Connecticut for over a year. Then in 1689 a new king took power in England. Andros was put in prison. The Connecticut charter was once again the law of the colony.

In the early 1700s most Connecticut people were farmers. Every town had a general store. Connecticut families loaded their wagons with corn and other crops. They traded with storekeepers for items they needed. But there were items they wanted from other places. They knew that they could ship out and sell some of their crops for those items. They decided to build ships for transporting products.

Many ships were built in such Connecticut towns as New Haven, New London, Norwich, and Hartford. Wood, food, tobacco, and cattle were shipped from Connecticut. Clothes, guns, and spices were brought back to Connecticut.

At Mystic Seaport visitors can see a rebuilt Connecticut whaling village of a hundred years ago.

Connecticut people also began to manufacture many items. In 1737 the first copper coins in America were made by Samuel Higley. He was a Simsbury blacksmith. Now some people could pay at stores with coins instead of crops. In 1740 Edward and William Pattison of Berlin made the first tinware in America. Soon Connecticut people were making tin pots, pans, and silverware. Connecticut also became a leader in clock making.

During the 1700s, "Yankee Peddlers" became well known in New England. They went from town to town selling buttons, hats, combs, clocks, and other Connecticut products. Nutmeg is a large seed used as a spice. It was said that clever Yankee Peddlers fooled people by selling *wooden* nutmegs. If they did that they had to get out of town fast—before their customers found out about it.

England took firmer control of the American Colonies after winning the French and Indian War in 1763.

In the 1760s many people in Connecticut—and the rest of the English colonies—became unhappy with English rule. They hated the taxes they had to pay the king. They didn't like being ruled by the king. They wanted freedom. They decided to form a new country—the United States of America.

The Revolutionary War (rev • oh • LOO • shun • airy wore) started in Massachusetts on April 19, 1775. Thousands of Connecticut men fought in George Washington's army.

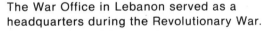

The War Office in Lebanon served as a headquarters during the Revolutionary War.

Fort Griswold
State Park
monument to
the soldiers
of the Revolution
who lost their
lives nearby.

There were no big battles in Connecticut. But there were fights at Stonington, Danbury, New Haven, and New London. At the Battle of Fort Griswold in Groton, the English killed American soldiers and townspeople. They also burned the town.

During the war, Connecticut supplied guns to George Washington's army. Governor Jonathan Trumbull saw to it that Connecticut also provided clothing and food for the army. Connecticut provided so much that George Washington later nicknamed it the *Provision* (pro • VIH • zhun) *State*.

Nathan Hale was a famous Revolutionary War hero. He was born in Coventry, Connecticut. He became a schoolteacher. When George Washington needed a spy to

Left: The schoolhouse in New London where Nathan
     Hale taught.
Above: The Nathan Hale Homestead in Coventry.

go into the New York area, Nathan Hale volunteered. He
pretended to be a Dutch schoolmaster. He learned what
George Washington wanted to know. But before Hale
could get back to his army, the English captured him. He
was sentenced to be hanged. Just before his death,
Nathan Hale made a famous speech. "I only regret that I
have but one life to lose for my country," he said. Nathan
Hale was only twenty-one years old when he died for his
country.

Above: A flag from the Revolutionary War, the
Connecticut 2nd Continental Dragoon.
Top right: Ethan Allan.
Right: Litchfield, where Ethan Allan was born.

Ethan Allen was another Revolutionary War hero. He
was born in Litchfield. He and about 80 soldiers known as
the *Green Mountain Boys* captured Fort Ticonderoga in
New York.

The Americans won the Revolutionary War in 1783. A
new country had been born—the United States of
America.

On January 9, 1788, Connecticut became the fifth state to join the United States. Connecticut had two capitals—Hartford and New Haven. State lawmakers met in Hartford in the spring. They met in New Haven in the fall. It wasn't until 1875 that Hartford became the only capital.

The new state had many nicknames. It was called the *Constitution* (con • stih • TOO • shun) *State* because its Fundamental Orders of 1639 were called the "first written constitution." It was nicknamed the *Nutmeg State* in memory of those Yankee Peddlers. Connecticut was called the *Land of Steady Habits* because its people were known for hard work and thrift. "Yankee Doodle," was a popular song during the Revolutionary War. It became the state song.

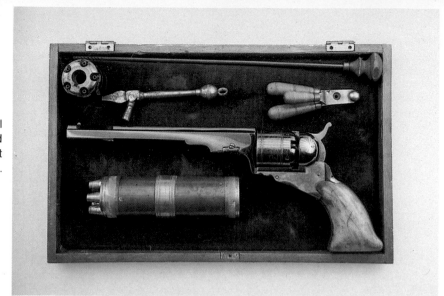

The Colt pistol was invented by Samuel Colt of Hartford.

About 1776 David Bushnell, from Westbrook, built a submarine. People laughed at Bushnell. They called his ship "Bushnell's Turtle." Now people call Bushnell the "father of the submarine."

In the 1800s many more inventions came out of Connecticut. A Yale man, Eli Whitney, built cotton gins. These machines made it easier to separate the cotton from the seed. In 1845 Elias (ee • LYE • us) Howe of New Hartford invented the first modern sewing machine. Samuel Colt of Hartford invented the repeating pistols. Soldiers—and Western gunfighters—used these six-shooters. Another Connecticut Yankee, Linus Yale of Stamford, invented the first modern lock in 1848. Many people believe that Eli Terry and Seth Thomas invented the first modern clocks. In 1839 a Naugatuck man, Charles Goodyear, found a process to make rubber stronger. He called it "vulcanization" (vul • can • ih • ZAY • shun). Tires and other rubber products are made this way today.

These inventors were important to Connecticut. In the 1800s, factories made clocks, sewing machines, guns, and other products that were invented in Connecticut. Connecticut was changing from a farming state to a manufacturing state.

Many Connnecticut people hated slavery. Before the Civil War, some helped black slaves escape to Canada on the *underground railroad*. This wasn't a railroad. And it wasn't underground. It was a series of houses and other hiding places where slaves could hide on their flight to freedom.

No Civil War battles were fought in Connecticut. During the war (1861-1865) the state sent 57,379 men to fight on the side of the North. During World War I (1914-1918), submarines were built in Groton. In 1917 the Navy opened the United States Submarine Base in Groton. During World War II (1939-1945) submarines built in Groton sank many warships. In 1954 the first nuclear-powered submarine, the *Nautilus* (NAW • tih • lus) was built at Groton. In 1958 it floated beneath the ice of the North Pole.

The United States Submarine Base at Groton

Connecticut factories helped launch America out into space as well as underwater. During World War II airplane engines were produced in Connecticut. During the 1960s, parts for spaceships were made in Connecticut. Supplies for astronauts were made there, too.

Connecticut had clean air and water and lovely countryside. People liked to vacation there. But by the 1970s factories had caused air and water pollution. State lawmakers worked to stop this pollution.

Today, Connecticut still has the beautiful scenery it had when only Indians lived there. Jet engines, helicopters, and many other products are made in its cities. It is also a tourist state where people like to vacation.

You have learned about some of the history of Connecticut. Now it is time for a trip—in words and pictures—through the Constitution State.

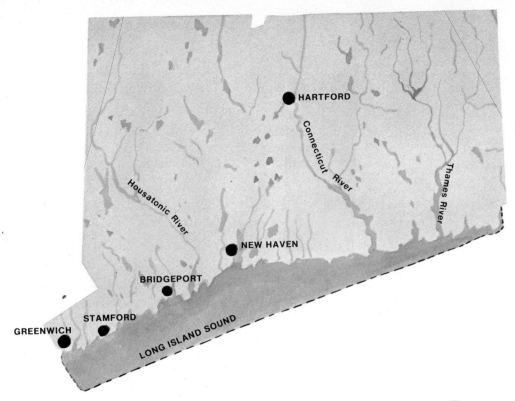

Connecticut is mainly a manufacturing state. That means many products are made in its cities.

The map shows that most of Connecticut's biggest cities are near water. Some cities are near rivers. Early settlers found that crops grew best in the river valleys. The water could be used for drinking.

Waterways could be used for travel. Many cities in southern Connecticut are near Long Island Sound. That body of water leads into the Atlantic Ocean. Many products still travel by boat along Connecticut waterways.

Bridgeport (BRIDJ • port) and Hartford (HEART • ferd) are Connecticut's biggest cities. Each city has about 153,000 people.

Hartford is a good place to begin your trip through Connecticut. Hartford is the capital of Connecticut. The city is on the west bank of the Connecticut River. It is near the center of the state.

Visit the state capitol building in Hartford. It looks like an old English castle. Inside this building men and women make laws for Connecticut. There is a statue of Nathan Hale inside the capitol building. It reminds us of Connecticut's history.

The state capitol building in Hartford

Modern Hartford is nicknamed the *Insurance City*. Many insurance companies have their headquarters in the city. Airplane parts, machinery, and chemicals are also made in Hartford. Many of Hartford's biggest buildings are downtown—in Constitution Plaza and the Hartford Civic Center.

Visit the Mark Twain House in Hartford. Twain was a famous writer. He lived there while he wrote such books as *Tom Sawyer, Huckleberry Finn,* and *A Connecticut Yankee in King Arthur's Court.* The Harriet Beecher Stowe (HAIR • ee • yet BEE • cher STOE) House is also in Hartford. She wrote *Uncle Tom's Cabin.* Noah Webster was born in West Hartford. He was a schoolteacher who wrote a famous dictionary. You can visit his birthplace.

You remember the Connecticut charter. You can see part of this charter. It is in the Connecticut State Library

Hartford's Constitution Plaza (left),
Civic Center (below left), and the
Mark Twain House (below)

Museum. The Connecticut Historical Society in Hartford has clocks and other items made in Connecticut long ago.

If you get tired of visiting museums, go to one of Hartford's lovely parks. One of the prettiest is Bushnell Park.

One of the most interesting places in the Hartford area is Dinosaur (DYE • nah • sore) State Park. It is in nearby Rocky Hill. There you can see dinosaur footprints made about 200 million years ago.

Waterbury (WATT • er • bury) is about 30 miles southwest of Hartford. It is Connecticut's fourth biggest city. The city lies on the Naugatuck (NAW • gah • tuck) River. Waterbury is nicknamed the *Brass Center of the World*. Waterbury makes more brass and copper products than any other city in the United States. Hardware, clocks, coins, buttons, and cartridges for bullets are some of these products.

New Haven

New Haven (NOO HAY • vin) is in southern Connecticut. It is near Long Island Sound. It is Connecticut's third biggest city. Long ago, Quinnipiac (quih • nih • PYE • ack) Indians lived in the New Haven area.

The first non-Indian settlers came to the region in 1638. They were led by Reverend John Davenport and Theophilus Eaton. The Indians sold land—including New Haven—for 23 coats, 12 spoons, 24 knives, 12 hatchets, scissors, farm tools, and some bowls. At first the settlers called their town *Quinnipiac*. They soon changed the name to New Haven, after a town in England.

New Haven is the home of one of the most famous schools in the world—Yale University. Nathan Hale, President William Howard Taft, and Noah Webster were just three of Yale's famous graduates.

New Haven is a cultural center. It has theaters, a fine symphony orchestra, and art museums. At the Peabody Museum of Natural History you can learn about Connecticut's dinosaur fossils.

Auto parts, guns, toys, and clothes are some of the products made in New Haven.

Phelps Gateway,
Yale University

Bridgeport is on Long Island Sound. It is about 18 miles southwest of New Haven. Hartford and Bridgeport are Connecticut's biggest cities. They have about the same number of people.

Once, Pequonnock (peh • KWAHN • ock) Indians lived in the Bridgeport area. In 1639 English settlers came to live there. They bought the land from the Indians for 30 bushels of corn and some blankets.

Bridgeport is the main manufacturing city in Connecticut. Machine tools are made there. So are electric and metal products, and ammunition.

Visit the P.T. Barnum Museum in Bridgeport. Phineas (FIN • ee • us) Taylor Barnum was once mayor of Bridgeport. But he was more famous as the creator of a circus. He called it *The Greatest Show on Earth.* Charles S. Stratton also lived in Bridgeport. He was only 28 inches tall as a young man. That isn't much taller than a new-born baby. But he was very smart. Barnum used him in his circus. Stratton was called "General Tom Thumb."

About 20 miles southwest of Bridgeport is Stamford. It is Connecticut's fifth biggest city. It is near the southwest corner of the state, on Long Island Sound.

Bridgeport, Hartford, New Haven, Waterbury, and Stamford (STAM • ferd) are Connecticut's five biggest cities. In cities across Connecticut, people make things for all of America. Here are some of the products they make:

Bloomfield (BLOOM • feeld): helicopters and airplanes
Bristol (BRISS • tuhl): clocks, ball bearings, auto parts, plastics
Danbury (DAN • bury): hats, metal products, drugs
East Hartford (EEST HEART • ferd): jet engines
Essex (ESS • ex): boats
Fairfield (FAIR • feeld): frozen foods, dairy products, radio and television sets
Greenwich (GREN • itch): switchboards, metal cans, fabrics, candy, perfumes, cigars
Groton (GROW • tun): submarines
Meriden (MARE • ih • din): silverware, electrical machinery, lumber
Mystic (MISS • tick): boats
New Britain (NOO BRIH • tin): hardware and other metal products
Norwalk (NOR • wawk): lights, tools, electronic equipment, chemicals, bread and other bakery products
North Haven (NORTH HAY • vin): jet engines, wire, nails, motorcycles, bicycles
Southington (SUTH • ing • tun): jet engines
Stratford (STRAT • ferd): helicopters, jet engines, metal products
West Hartford (WEST HEART • ferd): airplane engines
Windsor Locks (WIN • zer LOX): propellers, engines, draperies

The Whitfield House, Guilford

Long Island Sound separates the southern coast of Connecticut from the part of New York known as Long Island. You can visit many scenic places along the rocky southern coast of Connecticut.

From the town of Branford, you can take a boat trip on Long Island Sound. The boat goes to the Thimble Islands. There, the pirate Captain Kidd was supposed to have buried a treasure chest.

East of Branford is Guilford. There, you can visit the Whitfield House Museum. This house was built in 1639. It is the oldest stone house in the state.

Mystic Seaport

In years past, Connecticut sailors hunted whales. Visit famous Mystic Seaport. It looks just like a whaling village of over 100 years ago. There you can see a whaling ship, the *Charles W. Morgan*. You can also learn about shipbuilding and old-time fishermen.

As you travel through Connecticut, you'll see a lot of small towns and villages. Many have a pretty park known as a *village green*. They have churches, houses, and inns that are hundreds of years old.

Above: Keeler Tavern
Right: Pine Meadow village green

Forests still cover about 70 percent of Connecticut. The state also has areas of hills and low mountains. The wolves, moose, and bears that once lived in Connecticut's forests and mountains are gone. But foxes, muskrats, and minks can still be found in the state. Many birds— including orioles, sparrows, warblers, and ducks—live in the state. But most of them fly south in the winter. Connecticut gets snowy and cold in the winter.

Traveling through Connecticut, you'll also see many small lakes. And there are pretty waterfalls. One of them is Kent Falls, near Kent.

Some farming is still done in Connecticut. Tobacco is raised in the Connecticut Valley, near Hartford. Milk, eggs, chickens, apples, peaches, pears, and strawberries are other farm products.

Places can't tell the whole story of Connecticut. Many interesting people have lived in the Constitution State.

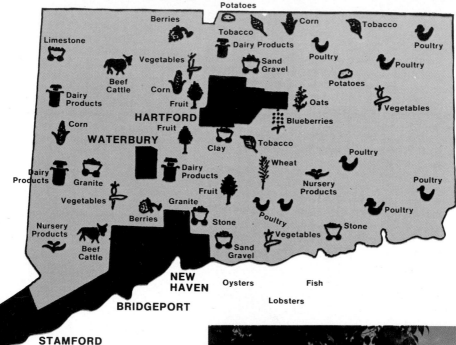

A farm in Northville

Katharine Hepburn was born in Hartford, in 1909. She became a famous actress. Other actors—including Paul Newman and Robert Mitchum—have lived in Connecticut. Connecticut people like the theater. The plays of William Shakespeare are performed at the American Shakespeare Theatre, in Stratford.

Ralph Nader was born in Winsted, in 1934. He became a lawyer. He wrote a book called *Unsafe At Any Speed*. In the book he said that cars weren't safe enough. He became a *consumer advocate* (con • SOO • mer ADD • vah • kit). That means he works to protect people from being cheated or endangered.

Ella Grasso was born in Windsor Locks in 1919. In 1974 she was elected governor of Connecticut. Women had been governors of other states before. But the others had followed their husbands as governor. Ms. Grasso was the *first* woman governor who won her office totally on her own merits.

Covered Bridge, West Cornwall

The land of the Pequot Indians . . . Dutch traders . . . the English . . . now the United States.

Home to "Yankee Peddlers" and inventors.

Birthplace of Nathan Hale and Ella Grasso.

A state filled with lovely villages . . . seacoast towns . . . and large manufacturing cities.

A state that produces helicopters . . . jet engines . . . and submarines.

This is Connecticut — the Constitution State.

Facts About CONNECTICUT

Area—About 5,009 square miles (48th biggest state)

Borders—Massachusetts on the north; Rhode Island on the east; Long Island Sound on the south; New York on the west

Greatest Distance North to South—75 miles

Greatest Distance East to West—90 miles

Highest Point—2,380 feet above sea level (Mount Frissell)

Lowest Point—Sea level (along Long Island Sound)

Hottest Recorded Temperature—105°F. (at Waterbury, on July 22, 1926)

Coldest Recorded Temperature—Minus 32°F. (at Falls Village on February 16, 1943)

Statehood—5th state, on January 9, 1788

Capital—Hartford

Counties—8

U.S. Senators—2

U.S. Representatives—6

Electoral Votes—8

State Senators—36

State Representatives—151

State Song—"Yankee Doodle"

State Motto— *Qui Transtulit Sustinet* (Latin for "He Who Transplanted Still Sustains")

Official Nickname—Constitution State

Other Nicknames—Nutmeg State, Provision State, Land of Steady Habits

Origin of Name Connecticut—From the Algonkian Indian phrase *Quinnehtukqut* meaning "upon the long river" or "on the long tidal river"

State Seal—Provided for in the constitution, 1818; adopted in 1931

State Flag—Adopted in 1897

State Flower—Mountain laurel

State Tree—White oak

State Bird—American robin

State Animal—Sperm whale

State Gem—Garnet

State Insect—Praying Mantis

Principal River—Connecticut River

Some Other Rivers—Housatonic, Naugatuck, Shepaug, Thames, Quinebaug, Pequonnock, Mad, Salmon, Weekeepeemee, Pootatuck

Farm Products—Milk and other dairy products, eggs, poultry, tobacco, apples, peaches, pears, strawberries

Manufacturing Products—Airplane engines, submarines, helicopters, boats, silverware, many metal products, electrical products, rubber products, foods

Mining—Stone, sand, gravel
Population—3,107,576 (1980 census; 25th most populous state)
Population Density—620 people per square mile
Population Distribution—77 percent urban
                                           23 percent rural
Major Cities—Bridgeport 142,546 (1980 census)
                 Hartford 136,392
                 New Haven 126,109
                 Waterbury 103,266
                 Stamford 102,453

Connecticut History

Hundreds of years before white people arrived, Indians of the Algonkian family of tribes lived in Connecticut

1614—Dutch explorer Adriaen Block sails up Connecticut River; Dutch claim Connecticut
1632—Englishman Edward Winslow explores Connecticut Valley
1633—The Dutch build a fur trading post at Hartford; the English build their first Connecticut settlement, at Windsor

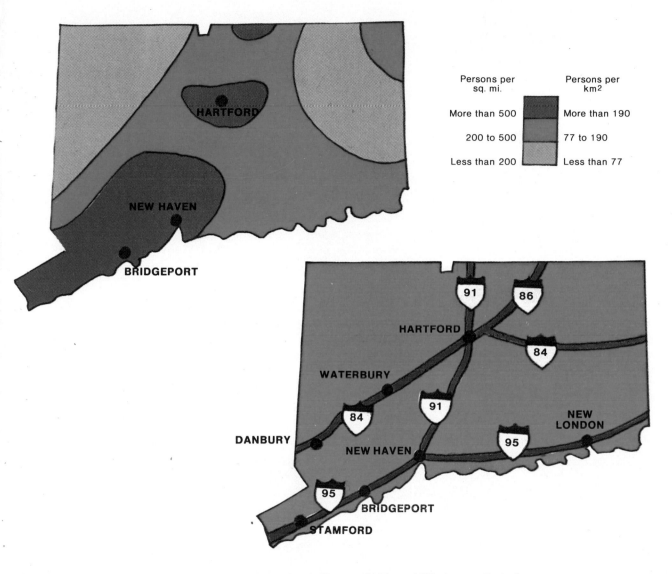

Persons per sq. mi. | Persons per km²
More than 500 | More than 190
200 to 500 | 77 to 190
Less than 200 | Less than 77

1636—Three River Towns of Hartford, Wethersfield, and Windsor unite to form
      Connecticut Colony
1637—Englishman John Mason and his army defeat Indians in Pequot War
1638—New Haven is founded
1639—The "first written constitution," the Fundamental Orders, adopted by
      the Connecticut Colony
1662—Connecticut Colony is officially chartered, becoming one of original
      thirteen English colonies
1665—New Haven becomes part of Connecticut Colony

1674—Dutch are driven out by English

1675-1678—King Philip's War ends major Indian fighting in Connecticut

1687—According to tradition, charter is hidden from Sir Edmund Andros in the Charter Oak

1701—Yale University founded

1737—First copper coins in America minted by Samuel Higley

1740—First tinware in America made by Edward and William Pattison

1750—First hat factory in America founded at Wethersfield

1763—At end of French and Indian War, England is in control of Connecticut

1775—Revolutionary War begins on April 19; Connecticut sends 31,939 men to fight in George Washington's Continental Army

1776—Nathan Hale is executed

1783—United States is born as Americans win Revolutionary War

1784—Slavery is abolished in Connecticut

1788—Connecticut becomes the fifth state on January 9

1794—Cotton gin patented by Eli Whitney

1800—Population of state is 250,902

1818—New state constitution is ratified

1837—First railroad trains operate in Connecticut

1839—Charles Goodyear of Naugatuck discovers vulcanization of rubber

1861-1865—During Civil War, 57,379 Connecticut men serve for the North

1875—Hartford becomes only capital

1888—Happy 100th birthday, Connecticut!

1888—Great Blizzard

1898—First car insurance in America is issued at Hartford

1900—Population is 908,420

1910—Coast Guard Academy is moved to New London

1914-1918—World War I; 60,000 Connecticut men serve

1917—United States Submarine Base is established at Groton

1939-1945—During World War II, 210,891 Connecticut men and women serve; state supplies submarines and airplane engines

1954—The first atomic submarine, the *Nautilus,* is launched at Groton

1965—Present state constitution is adopted

1966—Dinosaur tracks are found at Rocky Hill

1970—Population of Connecticut is 3,032,217

1974—Ella Grasso is elected governor

1978—Indians from Connecticut and five other states meet in Rhode Island as they try to regain some of their lands

1979—Grasso begins second term as governor

1981—William A. O'Neill is elected governor

INDEX

INDEX, Cont'd.

About the Author:

Dennis Fradin attended Northwestern University on a creative writing scholarship and graduated in 1967. While still at Northwestern, he published his first stories in *Ingenue* magazine and also won a prize in *Seventeen's* short story competition. A prolific writer, Dennis Fradin has been regularly publishing stories in such diverse places as *The Saturday Evening Post, Scholastic, National Humane Review, Midwest,* and *The Teaching Paper.* He has also scripted several educational films. Since 1970 he has taught second grade reading in a Chicago school—a rewarding job, which, the author says, "provides a captive audience on whom I test my children's stories." Married and the father of three children, Dennis Fradin spends his free time with his family or playing a myriad of sports and games with his childhood chums.

About the Artists:

Len Meents studied painting and drawing at Southern Illinois University and after graduation in 1969 he moved to Chicago. Mr. Meents works full time as a painter and illustrator. He and his wife and child currently make their home in LaGrange, Illinois.

Richard Wahl, graduate of the Art Center College of Design in Los Angeles, has illustrated a number of magazine articles and booklets. He is a skilled artist and photographer who advocates realistic interpretations of his subjects. He lives with his wife and two sons in Libertyville, Illinois.